The Four Questions

Also by Byron Katie

A Friendly Universe

The Four Questions

For Henny Penny and Anybody with Stressful Thoughts

BYRON KATIE
with
HANS WILHELM

Illustrated by Hans Wilhelm

A TarcherPerigee Book

One day when Henny Penny was scratching about for something tasty to nibble, an acorn fell—**SMACK**—on her head.

"Goodness gracious me!" cried Henny Penny.

*"HELP, HELP!
THE SKY IS FALLING!
THE SKY IS FALLING!"*

Cocky Locky had heard it all before. Henny Penny wasn't the brightest chick in his coop.

"Now, now, Henny Penny," he said calmly. "The sky is falling—is that true?"

"YES, YES! OF COURSE!" said Henny Penny. "Look at this awful bump on my head!"

Then Ducky Lucky said, "Henny Penny, can you absolutely know that it's true that the sky is falling?"

"What do you mean?" said Henny Penny. "Hmm. I *think* it was the sky. Oh, dear, now I'm totally confused."

"Well, Henny Penny," said Goosey Loosey,
"how do you feel when you think the sky is falling?"

"Oh goodness gracious me," wailed Henny Penny.

"I'M SHAKING IN MY FEATHERS.
I'M TREMBLING IN FEAR.
MY NERVES ARE ALL SHOT.
I'M TOTALLY BESIDE MYSELF.
I'M SCARED SILLY.
I'M FRIGHTENED AND FLUSTERED,
TERRIFIED AND TROUBLED.
IN SHORT: I'M ALL CHICKEN AND
NEVER FELT WORSE!"

"Okay, okay!" said Turkey Lurkey. "Who would you be without the thought that the sky is falling, even though you have a bump on your head?"

"Oh my!" Henny Penny laughed, feeling a sudden surge of energy.

"I would be such a different chicken:
I would be calm, cool, and collected.
Nothing could ruffle my feathers.
No worries could touch me.
I would see that my life is hunky-dory.
I would have the whole world at my wingtips.

I would be happy as a lark.
I would be the most amazing
chicken ever—bump and all!"

Foxy Loxy came up to them now. He had listened to the whole cackle.

"Now, Henny Penny," he said, "I hear that you believed the sky was falling. What wonderful things would happen if that were true? Give us three reasons why, if the sky fell, that could be a good thing."

"A good thing?! The sky falling?!" said Henny Penny. "I never thought of that. Hmm. Let me see."

"Well, if the sky has fallen, we wouldn't have to worry about it falling anymore. We could just get on with our business."

"**Very good,**" said Foxy Loxy.

"There would be no more dark clouds, storms, or lightning!"

"**Excellent**," said Foxy Loxy.

"If the sky has fallen, we could all see without limit, even beyond the sky!"

"*Wouldn't that be a wonderful sight!*" said Foxy Loxy.

"Oh goodness!" said Henny Penny. "I feel *so* much better now!"

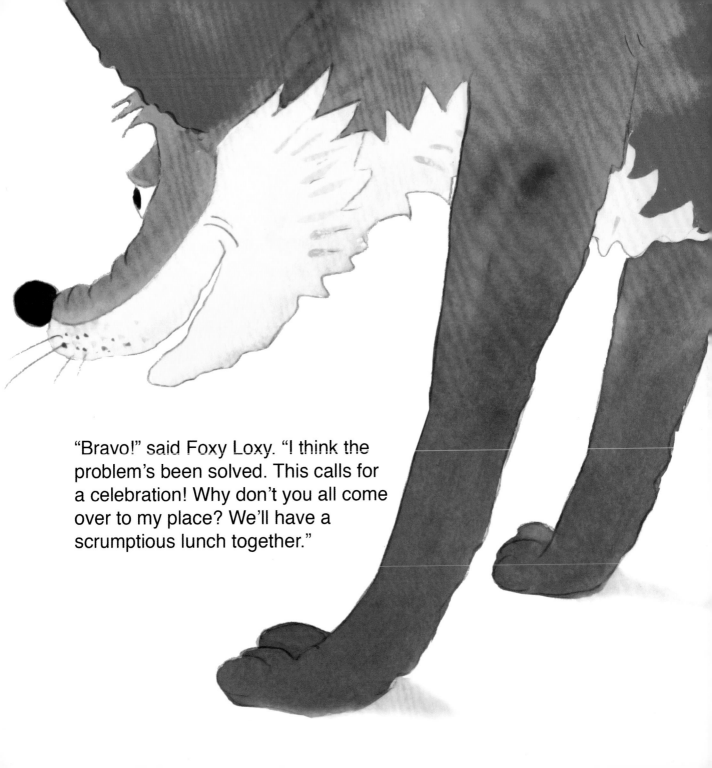

"Bravo!" said Foxy Loxy. "I think the problem's been solved. This calls for a celebration! Why don't you all come over to my place? We'll have a scrumptious lunch together."

"Wonderful idea!" said Cocky Locky.

"Thank you so much!" said Ducky Lucky.

"Very kind of you!" said Goosey Loosey.

"I'm really hungry!" said Turkey Lurkey.

"Just follow me," said Foxy Loxy, licking his chops.

Henny Penny said nothing.
She thought for a moment,
and then for another moment,
and then she shouted:

"HOLD IT!!!!

A FOX INVITING A CHICKEN, A ROOSTER, A DUCK, A GOOSE, AND A TURKEY FOR LUNCH???

GET REAL!!!!

THIS IS A GOOD IDEA?

CAN WE ABSOLUTELY KNOW THAT THAT'S TRUE?"

"DRAT!"

In the end, Foxy Loxy had a grilled cheese sandwich.
But it just didn't taste the same.

A Note from Byron Katie

Well done, Henny Penny! This anxious little chicken discovered that questioning her fearful thoughts could save lives. Freedom is as simple as asking yourself four simple questions whenever you want to turn your fears around.

The Work, which forms the basis of this story, is a way to identify and question the thoughts that cause all the fear and unhappiness in your child's life. It's a way to find peace in your life as well. The old, the young, the sick, the healthy, the educated, the uneducated—anyone with an open mind can do this Work.

Those of you who are interested in learning how to do The Work, yourselves or with your children, will find everything you need to know in my book *Loving What Is* or on my website, www.thework.com.

Since the beginning of time, people have been trying to change the world so they can be happy. This hasn't ever worked, because it approaches the problem backward. What The Work gives us is a way to change the projector—mind—rather than the projected. It's like when there's a piece of lint on a projector's lens. We think there's a flaw on the screen, and we try to change this person and that person, whomever the flaw appears to be on next. But it's futile to try to change the projected images. Once we realize where the lint is, we can clear the lens itself. This is the end of suffering.

The Four Questions and Turnarounds

1. Is it true?
2. Can you absolutely know that it's true?
3. How do you react, what happens, when you believe that thought?
4. Who would you be without the thought?
   and
   Turn the thought around to its opposites, and identify at least three specific, genuine examples of how each turnaround is true.

Peace to you and your children,

Byron Katie

tarcherperigee

An imprint of Penguin Random House LLC
375 Hudson Street
New York, New York 10014

Most Tarcher/Penguin books are available at special quantity discounts for bulk purchase for sales promotions, premiums, fund-raising, and educational needs. Special books or book excerpts also can be created to fit specific needs. For details, write: SpecialMarkets@penguinrandomhouse.com.

ISBN 9780399174247

Printed in China
10 9 8 7 6 5 4 3 2 1